D1124643

MOTORSPORTS MANIACS

LAWN MOWER RACING

BY KATE MIKOLEY

Gareth Stevens
PUBLISHING

Please visit our website, www.garethstevens.com. For a free color catalog of all our high-quality books, call toll free 1-800-542-2595 or fax 1-877-542-2596.

Cataloging-in-Publication Data

Names: Mikoley, Kate.
Title: Lawn mower racing / Kate Mikoley.
Description: New York : Gareth Stevens Publishing, 2020. | Series: Motorsports maniacs | Includes glossary and index.
Identifiers: ISBN 9781538240861 (pbk.) | ISBN 9781538240885 (library bound) | ISBN 9781538240878 (6 pack)
Subjects: LCSH: Riding lawn mowers--Juvenile literature. | Racing--Juvenile literature. | Contests--Juvenile literature.
Classification: LCC SB433.2 M63 2020 | DDC 629.228--dc23

First Edition

Published in 2020 by
Gareth Stevens Publishing
111 East 14th Street, Suite 349
New York, NY 10003

Designer: Sarah Liddell
Editor: Kate Mikoley

Photo credits: Cover, p. 1 Barcroft/Contributor/Barcroft Media/Getty Images; dirt background used throughout Yibo Wang/Shutterstock.com; tire mark texture used throughout Slay/Shutterstock.com; p. 5 Anne Hawken/Contributor/Moment Mobile/Getty Images; pp. 7, 17, 21, 27 Andrew Matthews - PA Images/Contributor/PA Images/Getty Images; p. 9 Johnathan Ferrey/Stringer/Getty Images Sport/Getty Images; pp. 11, 13 Phil Cole/Staff/Getty Images Sport/Getty Images; p. 15 (main) Split Second/Contributor/Corbis Sport/Getty Images; p. 15 (inset) anouk3/Shutterstock.com; p. 19 Ralf Geithe/Shutterstock.com; p. 23 Steve Parsons - PA Images/PA Images/Getty Images; p. 25 The Washington Post/Contributor/The Washington Post/Getty Images; p. 29 Oliver Foerstner/Shutterstock.com.

Printed in the United States of America

CPSIA compliance information: Batch #CS19GS: For further information contact Gareth Stevens, New York, New York at 1-800-542-2595.

CONTENTS

RACING MOWERS

Lawn mowers are machines used to cut grass. Chances are you've seen someone using one before. But have you ever seen someone racing with one? It's not as uncommon as it sounds. Many people love lawn mower racing!

TEST DRIVE

IN LAWN MOWER RACING, RIDING LAWN MOWERS ARE COMMONLY USED. THIS IS A KIND OF MOWER WITH A SEAT. THE DRIVER SITS ON TOP AND USES A **STEERING WHEEL** TO DIRECT THE MOWER.

Lawn mower races often take place at community events, such as fairs. The tracks are commonly 0.1 mile (0.16 km). Racers do 10 laps around the track to decide their starting position in the finals. The final event is 20 laps.

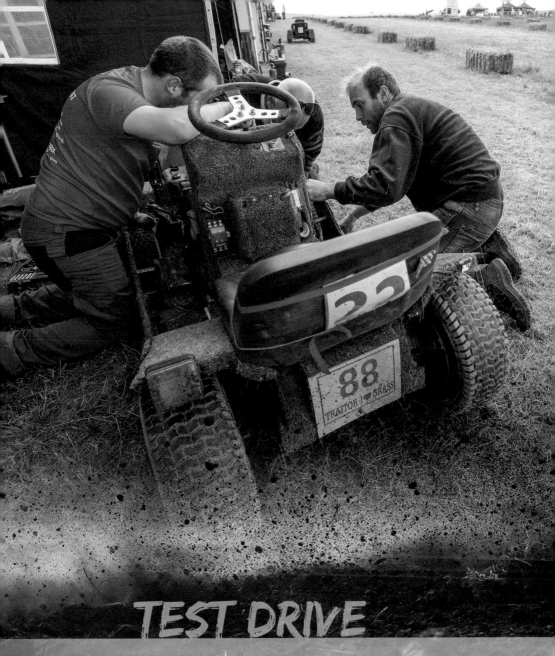

TEST DRIVE

BEFORE A RIDER CAN TAKE PART IN THE RACE, THEIR MOWER MUST PASS AN **INSPECTION** TO MAKE SURE IT'S SAFE TO RACE.

DON'T CUT THE GRASS!

Lawn mowers use sharp blades to cut grass. In lawn mower racing, the mower doesn't need to be able to cut grass. The blades are removed from racing mowers. This way, if there's a crash, no one will get hurt by the blades.

TEST DRIVE

MANY LAWN MOWER RACES AREN'T
HELD ON GRASS AT ALL, BUT RATHER
ON DIRT OR CLAY TRACKS.

ALL ABOUT THE SPEED

Not all racing mowers are the same. Some are just like the ones that would be used to mow a lawn, but the blades have been removed. Others have had lots of changes made to them and can go super fast!

TEST DRIVE

DIFFERENT KINDS OF MOWERS RACE IN
DIFFERENT CLASSES, OR GROUPS. MOWERS THAT
HAVE HAD LOTS OF CHANGES RACE IN DIFFERENT
CLASSES THAN THOSE THAT HAVEN'T.

If you've seen an adult cutting the lawn with a riding mower, they were probably moving at around 5 miles (8 km) per hour. In lawn mower racing, some mowers can get up to 60 miles (97 km) per hour!

TEST DRIVE

LAWN MOWER RACERS MAKE CHANGES
THAT MAKE THEIR MOWERS GO FASTER. THIS
SHOULD NEVER BE DONE WITH REGULAR
LAWN MOWERS USED TO CUT GRASS.

MAKING CHANGES

As long as a mower was originally made to cut grass, it can be used in a lawn mower race. Racers can change out different parts, such as the **engine**, but in most cases, they must still use parts that were made for lawn mowers.

GO-KART

TEST DRIVE

RACERS CAN ADD STRONGER WHEELS,
SUCH AS THOSE COMMONLY USED ON
GO-KARTS, TO THEIR MOWERS.

Some motorsports cost a lot of money. Lawn mower racing is often cheaper because racers don't have to buy pricey **vehicles**. It's suggested to use a lawn mower you already have and spend any money on changes to make it better for race day!

TEST DRIVE

WORKING ON THE MOWER CAN BE JUST AS FUN AS RACING IT. MANY RACERS ENJOY BEING **CREATIVE** AND FINDING NEW WAYS TO MAKE THEIR MOWERS GO FAST.

STAYING SAFE

There are sometimes crashes—and even broken bones—in lawn mower racing. It's important for drivers to stay safe. All riders should wear helmets and a special piece of gear that keeps the neck safe.

TEST DRIVE

DRIVERS SHOULD WEAR
LONG SLEEVES, LONG PANTS, AND
GLOVES WHILE RACING.

Another important safety tool required in races is called a tethered kill switch. This **cord** is fixed to both the driver and the mower. If the driver falls off the mower, it will turn off the engine and stop the mower.

TEST DRIVE

WITHOUT A TETHERED KILL SWITCH, THE
MOWER COULD KEEP MOVING EVEN AFTER THE
DRIVER FELL OFF AND WOULD BE A DANGER
TO EVERYONE AT THE RACE.

LAWN MOWER RACING HISTORY

Lawn mower racing has been happening for **decades**! The oldest riding lawn mower race in the United States still happens every year in Twelve Mile, Indiana. The event, held on the Fourth of July, was first held in 1963.

TEST DRIVE

LAWN MOWER RACING ALSO HAPPENS
IN OTHER PARTS OF THE WORLD. IN 1973, THE
BRITISH LAWN MOWER RACING ASSOCIATION
WAS STARTED IN ENGLAND.

KEEPING AN EYE ON THE RACE

The United States Lawn Mower Racing Association (USLMRA) is the oldest and biggest group that governs lawn mower races in the United States. Formed in 1992, the group oversees more than 800 lawn mower racers across the country.

TEST DRIVE

THE AMERICAN RACING MOWER ASSOCIATION (ARMA) IS ANOTHER GROUP THAT OVERSEES LAWN MOWER RACES. THERE ARE ALSO MANY SMALLER LOCAL GROUPS.

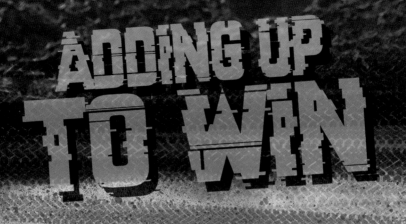

ADDING UP TO WIN

The USLMRA awards points to winners of each event. At the end of a season, racers with the most points become "points winners." Some other groups do this, too. Since there are multiple groups that govern lawn mower races, the rules may sometimes be a little different.

TEST DRIVE

WINNERS GET **TROPHIES**, BUT UNLIKE OTHER SPORTING EVENTS, LAWN MOWER RACERS DON'T RACE FOR MONEY.

ALL ABOUT THE FUN!

By not racing for money, groups are able to keep lawn mower racing a generally low-cost motorsport. For most racers, the fun isn't about money—it's about having a good time and being with friends.

TEST DRIVE

LAWN MOWER RACING EVEN HAS
A HALL OF FAME! THE USLMRA NATIONAL
LAWN MOWER RACING HALL OF FAME
IS IN MARION, OHIO.

LAWN MOWER RACING SAFETY TIPS

ALL LAWN MOWER RACERS SHOULD:

- MAKE SURE BLADES ARE REMOVED FROM THEIR MOWERS

- WEAR A HELMET AND A NECK SUPPORT DEVICE

- WEAR A LONG-SLEEVED SHIRT, LONG PANTS, AND GLOVES

- USE A TETHERED KILL SWITCH

- KNOW AND FOLLOW THE RULES OF THE RACE THEY'RE TAKING PART IN

- USE A MOWER THAT IS IN GOOD CONDITION AND PASSES INSPECTION

FOR MORE INFORMATION

BOOKS

Levit, Joe. *Motorsports Trivia: What You Never Knew About Car Racing, Monster Truck Events, and More Motor Mania.* North Mankato, MN: Capstone Press, 2019.

Mapua, Jeff. *Extreme Motorsports.* New York, NY: Rosen Publishing, 2016.

Omoth, Tyler. *Incredible Car Stunts.* North Mankato, MN: Capstone Press, 2016.

WEBSITES

The United States Lawn Mower Racing Association
letsmow.com
Learn all about this extreme motorsport on the USLMRA's official website.

Wisconsin Lawn Mower Racing Association
wisconsinlawnmowerracing.com
View photos and read about a local chapter of the USLMRA.

GLOSSARY

cord: a long object similar to a rope, but usually thinner than a rope and thicker than a string

creative: being able to make new things and come up with new ideas

decade: a period of 10 years

engine: a machine that makes power

inspection: an official check to make sure something is in working order

steering wheel: a wheel that a driver uses to control the direction of a vehicle

trophy: a prize awarded to the winner of a race

vehicle: an object that moves people from one place to another, such as a car

INDEX